SCIENCE FACTORY
AIR AND FLIGHT

JON RICHARDS

FRANKLIN WATTS
LONDON • SYDNEY

© Aladdin Books Ltd 1999

Designed and produced by
Aladdin Books Ltd
28 Percy Street
London W1P 0LD

ISBN 0 7496 3410 3 (hardcover)
ISBN 0 7496 4715 9 (paperback)

First published in Great Britain
in 1999 by
Franklin Watts Books
96 Leonard Street
London EC2A 4RH

Design

David West
Children's Book Design

Designer
Flick Killerby

Illustrator
Ian Thompson

Printed in the U.A.E.

A CIP catalogue entry for this book is
available from the British Library.

Some of the illustrations in this series
have appeared in previous books
published by Aladdin Books.

The author, Jon Richards, has written
a number of science and technology
books for children.

Steve Parker, the consultant, has
worked on more than 150 books for
children, mainly on a science theme.

All the photos in this book were
taken by Roger Vlitos.

INTRODUCTION

You can't see it, but air is one of the most important things in your life. It is made up of a mixture of gases which lie around the Earth in a layer called the atmosphere. Not only do you breathe air in to keep you alive, but it is used to push boats and it can even help planes to fly through the sky. Read on and discover a host of experiments, as well as the 'why-it-works' boxes which will teach you more about the power of air!

CONTENTS

THE WORKSHOP

BEFORE YOU START any of the experiments, it is important that you learn a few simple rules about the care of your science factory.

● Always keep your hands and the work surfaces clean. Dirt can damage results and ruin an experiment!

● Read the instructions carefully before you start each experiment.

● Make sure you have all the equipment you need for the experiment (see checklist opposite).

● If you don't have the right piece of equipment, then improvise. For example, a washing-up liquid bottle will do just as well as a plastic drinks bottle.

● Don't be afraid to make mistakes. Just start again – patience is very important!

Equipment checklist:
● Scissors, tape and glue
  Hair-dryer
Plastic bottles and fruit-juice cartons
Glass jars and cardboard boxes
Table-tennis balls
Toy cars
Paper, card and tissue paper
Modelling clay
Ribbons
        ● Aluminium foil
        ● Wire
        ● Ballpoint pens
        ● Drinking straws and balloons
        ● Plastic cups and tubs
        ● Toothpicks, sticks and
matchsticks
        ● Cotton thread
Elastic bands

WARNING:
Some of the experiments in this book need the
      help of an adult. Always ask a grown-up to give you
            a hand when you are using scissors or
              electrical objects such as hair-dryers!

GOING UP

WHAT YOU
NEED
*Aluminium
foil
Thin card
Cotton thread
Modelling clay
Tape
Stick*

WINDS AND WEATHER ON THE EARTH ARE CAUSED BY DIFFERENCES IN AIR TEMPERATURE. Heat from the Sun warms the ground in one spot, which, in turn, warms the air just above it. As this air is warmed, it expands, becoming lighter or less dense. This less-dense air rises, forming air currents, or winds. You can copy and see these air movements on a smaller scale using some foil shapes and a heater.

Watch as your aluminium foil shapes twirl in the warm air rising from the heater.

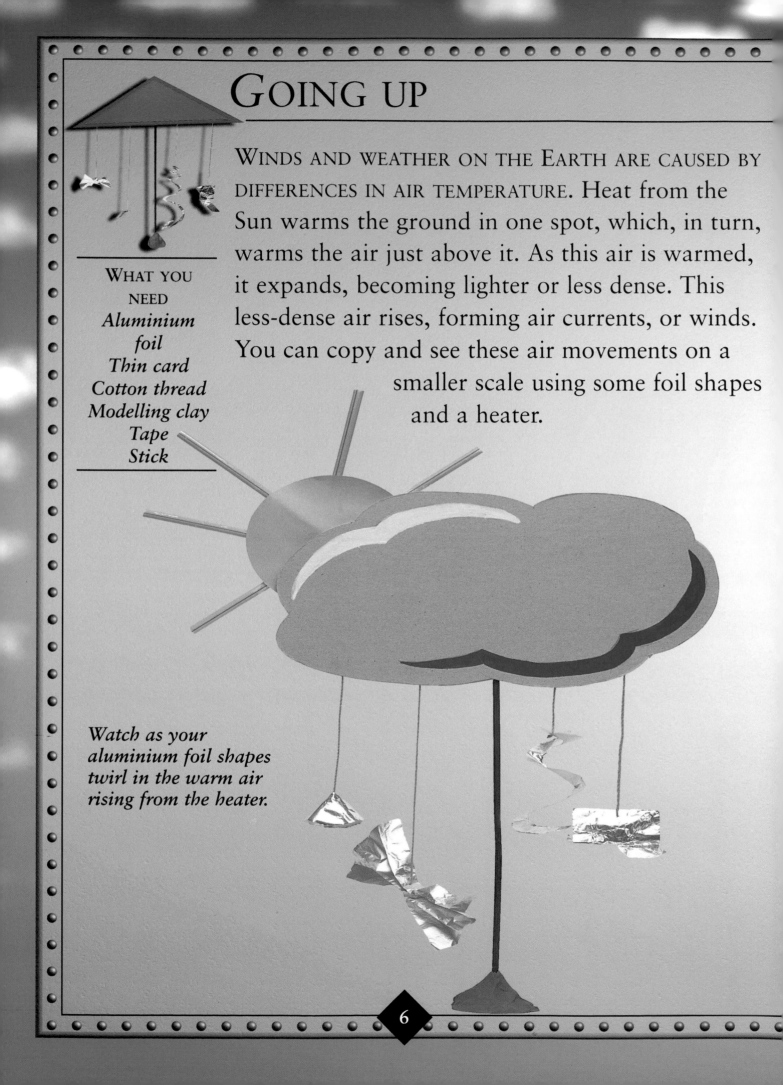

MOBILE AIR

1 Cut some strips of aluminium foil into shapes.

2 Attach a length of cotton thread to each foil shape.

3 Cut a large cloud shape out of card, fix it to a stick and secure a piece of modelling clay to the base. Make sure that it will stand up.

4 Attach the foil shapes to the card cloud and place your mobile above a heater – keep it away from any flames.

WHY IT WORKS

Air above the heater is warmed, becomes less dense and starts to rise. This rising warm air pushes against your foil shapes, causing them to turn.

DIRECTION OF MOVEMENT

ALUMINIUM SHAPES DEFLECTED BY WARM AIR

ALUMINIUM SHAPES

RISING WARM AIR

ALL SHAPES AND SIZES

See how well some other foil shapes spin. You will find that some shapes spin better because they are deflected more easily by the rising warm air.

TWISTED LOOP

CURVE

HOT-AIR BALLOON

BECAUSE HOT AIR RISES (SEE PAGES 6-7), it can be used to lift things into the air. For more than 200 years, people have flown through the air in hot-air balloons. The first hot-air balloon was built in 1783 by two French brothers, Joseph and Jaques Montgolfier. This experiment shows how to build your own miniature hot-air balloon and how it can fly.

WHAT YOU NEED

Tissue paper
Glue
Card
Cotton thread
Hair-dryer

UP, UP AND AWAY

1 Fold a sheet of tissue paper in half and cut out one panel for your hot-air balloon.

2 Repeat this using different colours of tissue paper, until you have cut out four panels.

3 Glue the edges of your panels together to make your balloon.

4 Fold a piece of card to make a small basket and attach it to the bottom of your balloon using four lengths of cotton thread.

WHY IT WORKS

WARM AIR INSIDE THE BALLOON

The air inside your balloon is warmer and less dense than the air outside it. As a result, this air inside the balloon rises, carrying the balloon up with it.

5 Blow the balloon up with hot air from a hair-dryer. Watch it rise from the ground.

GETTING HEAVY

Make some figures out of modelling clay and place them inside the balloon's basket. You will find that the more weight the balloon has to carry, the harder it will be to fly.

SAILING AWAY

WHAT YOU NEED
Plastic bottle
Thin card
Drinking straw
Modelling clay
Fruit-juice carton

FOR THOUSANDS OF YEARS, sailors have been using the wind to push their boats along. Although engines and propellers are more widely used today, some boats, from small yachts to larger cruise liners, are still fitted with wind-catching sails. Make your own yacht and see how a sail catches the wind.

Float your boat in a bathtub full of water. Turn the sail so that it has its back to you while the boat points in another direction. Blow hard on the sail and watch the boat travel in the direction which the boat is pointing.

SAIL POWER

1 Cut a rectangular piece out of the side of a plastic bottle to make your boat's body.

2 Fix a lump of modelling clay in the bottom of your boat and use it to hold a straw mast.

3 Cut a triangular piece of paper to make a sail and pierce two holes in it to thread your mast through.

4 Cut out a wedge-shaped piece from a fruit-juice carton – this will be your keel. Fix a lump of modelling clay to each end and stick the keel to the boat's bottom.

WHY IT WORKS

As the wind catches the sail it tries to push the boat sideways. However, the resistance of the water on the keel stops the boat from going sideways. Instead the boat is pushed forwards.

DIRECTION OF BOAT'S TRAVEL

SAIL

DIRECTION OF WIND

KEEL

WATER RESISTANCE

MOVING YOUR SAILS

Try moving the position of your sail. You will find that the boat moves with less control when the sail is moved away from above the keel.

SAIL FIXED AT FRONT

SAIL FIXED AT REAR

TELLING THE WEATHER

EVEN THOUGH YOU CAN'T SEE IT, air has weight. The tiny molecules which make up air are attracted to the Earth by gravity, making them press on you. This is called air pressure. Air pressure is changing all the time, as air currents move over the planet and the weather changes. You can make a device which measures these changes in air pressure – it's called a barometer.

What you need
Glass jar
Thin card
Drinking straw
Toothpick
Balloon
Elastic band

RAIN OR SHINE?

1 *Cut the neck off a balloon and stretch the balloon over a glass jar. Secure the balloon with an elastic band.*

2 *Tape a toothpick to the end of a straw and tape the other end of the straw to the centre of the balloon lid.*

3 *Fold a sheet of card and fix a card triangle to the back to support it. Fix a pressure chart in place showing good weather at the top and bad weather at the bottom.*

FEEL THE PRESSURE

Try to lever up some paper using a ruler. Air pressure on the paper will make this quite hard. You can see the weight of air by balancing two full balloons, then emptying one.

AIR PRESSURE

FORCE

FULL BALLOON

EMPTY BALLOON

4 Put the barometer in front of the chart and mark where the pointer moves up and down over a few days.

WHY IT WORKS

Changes in air pressure will cause the balloon lid to bend, moving the pointer. A rise in air pressure is a sign of good weather, and a fall in air pressure is a sign of bad weather.

HIGHER AIR PRESSURE PUSHES DOWN ON THE BALLOON

POINTER RISES

POINTER FALLS

LOWER AIR PRESSURE CAUSES THE BALLOON TO BEND OUT

FALLING PRESSURE

HAVE YOU NOTICED HOW FAST-MOVING OBJECTS, such as cars and trains, seem to pull objects after them when they race by? This is because these fast objects push air along quickly. As the objects push air along, they create low pressure behind them, and air from around the sides is sucked in to equal out the difference in pressure. You can see this effect in action with this experiment.

WHAT YOU NEED
Two table-tennis balls
Two straws
Modelling clay
Hair-dryer

BLOWING BALLS

1 Stick small lumps of modelling clay to the ends of two drinking straws. The best straws to use are the flexible type with the crinkled section.

2 Attach table-tennis balls onto the modelling clay at the ends of the straws farthest from the crinkled section. Stick the other ends of the straws onto a flat surface, making sure that the straws can stand up.

14

AIR SQUEEZE

Blow between two sheets of paper. The low air pressure created by your blowing causes the sheets to come together.

WHY IT WORKS

The fast-moving air flowing between the two balls creates an area of low pressure between the balls. The balls are then pushed together by higher air pressure outside them.

FAST MOVING AIR

HIGHER PRESSURE

BALLS MOVE TOGETHER

LOWER AIR PRESSURE BETWEEN BALLS

3 *Blow downward onto the balls using a hair-dryer and watch as the two balls move towards each other.*

RISING PAPER

Blow over the surface of a piece of paper held by your mouth. The air you blow out creates an area of low air pressure above the paper, which causes the paper to rise.

FLOATING ON AIR

SOME VEHICLES, SUCH AS HOVERCRAFT, travel on top of a cushion of air. This removes any friction between the vehicle and the surface. Friction is a force between surfaces which can slow a vehicle down, making it harder for it to move. Build your own hovercraft and see how it moves about with little effort.

WHAT YOU NEED
Plastic tub
Hair-dryer

SPEEDY HOVERCRAFT

1 Take a clean, light-weight plastic tub and cut a hole in its base – this will be your hovercraft. Decorate the hovercraft as you like.

2 Place your hovercraft on a smooth surface. Blow air from a hair-dryer into the hole and watch as your hovercraft starts to float on a cushion of air. Now try pushing your hovercraft – notice how easily it glides around.

ADDING TO THE WEIGHT

Try adding some coins to the top of your hovercraft and see how this affects its movement. You will find that the heavier your hovercraft becomes, the more air is needed to lift it and the harder it becomes for it to move about.

COINS

WHY IT WORKS

As the hovercraft rises on a cushion of air, it no longer rubs against the surface. There is no longer any friction between the hovercraft and the surface, and the hovercraft can move easily.

AIR FROM HAIR-DRYER

TUB RISES ON A CUSHION OF AIR

HOVERCRAFT

AIR FORCES ITS WAY OUT, MAKING A CUSHION OF AIR WHICH THE TUB RIDES ON.

SHARP SHAPE

WHAT YOU NEED
Two identical toy cars
Thin card
Tape
Hair-dryer

HAVE YOU NOTICED THAT FAST RACING CARS ARE VERY POINTED? This streamlined shape lets them move through the air more easily and quickly. On the other hand, objects with an unstreamlined shape can be slowed down as they travel through the air. These experiments will show you how an object's shape can affect its movement.

The car covered by the curved card will experience less air resistance and will travel down the ramp faster than the other car.

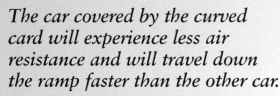

SLOWING THE FALL

Make a parachute by tying some cotton thread to four corners of a handkerchief. Fix a lump of modelling clay to the other ends of the cotton thread and throw it in the air. The parachute slows its fall because it traps air molecules under it, creating air resistance.

WHY IT WORKS

The car with the curved card travels faster because its shape disturbs the air less. The car with the unstreamlined body disturbs the air. This disturbed air increases the force called drag which slows the car down.

AIR MOVES OVER EASILY

DRAG

SQUARED FRONT

STREAMLINED SHAPE

DISTURBED AIR

STREAMLINED SHAPES

1 Take two identical model cars. Make sure that each moves as easily as the other. Cut out card rectangles which will cover the cars.

2 Attach the rectangles to the front of the cars. Fold one smoothly over the top to form a curve and bend the other one to form a right angle.

3 Tilt a board on a book to form a ramp. Release the cars from the top of the ramp at the same time into a wind caused by the hair-dryer.

TESTING TIME

When designers are testing the shapes of new cars, planes and rockets, they use wind tunnels to see how air will pass over the shapes. Trails of smoke are blown over the objects to show this more clearly. Build your own wind tunnel and test the shapes of different objects.

WHAT YOU NEED
Cardboard box
Sticks
Ribbons
Hair-dryer

WIND TUNNEL

1 Make a backdrop for your wind tunnel using a cardboard box and two triangular bases.

2 Cut slits in the base of the box and slide the two bases in to hold the box upright.

3 Carefully make holes in the centre of the box and push two thin sticks through them. These sticks will support objects which you are testing in your wind tunnel.

TESTING TIME

See how the two cars you used in the experiment on pages 18-19 test out in your wind tunnel.

4 Fix two ribbons to each side of a hairdryer. With the dryer on 'cool' setting, watch how the ribbons blow over a number of objects, such as a wing section (aerofoil – see pages 22-23) and a ball.

WHY IT WORKS

The air will pass over streamlined objects easily without causing much drag (see pages 18-19). However, unstreamlined shapes, such as the ball, will disturb the air flow, making the ribbons flap about.

WIND TUNNEL

AEROFOIL

FLYING WINGS

BIRDS AND AIRCRAFT STAY IN THE AIR BECAUSE OF THE SHAPE OF THEIR WINGS. This special shape is called an aerofoil. An aerofoil is flat on the bottom and curved on the top. This experiment will show you how this shape causes a wing to rise as air passes over it.

WHAT YOU NEED
Thin card
Tape
Two straws
Cotton thread
Hair-dryer

AEROFOIL

1 Fold a rectangular piece of card in two, leaving a slight overlap.

2 Push the overlapping ends together so that one side of the folded card is now curved.

3 Tape the ends of the card together to form your wing. Ask an adult to pierce holes at either end of your wing, using a knitting needle or a sharp pencil.

4 Now push a drinking straw through each pair of holes.

5 Pass lengths of cotton thread through each straw and pull them tight. Make sure the curved edge of your wing is on top.

6 Lift the wing a little and aim a hair-dryer at the folded edge. Turn on the hair-dryer, release the wing and watch it rise.

WHY IT WORKS

Because the wing is curved on top and flat underneath, air flowing over the wing has farther to travel – so it has to flow faster. Faster flowing air has less pressure (see pages 14-15). The higher pressure below the wing then pushes the wing up.

LOW PRESSURE ABOVE THE WING

WING RISES

HIGH PRESSURE BELOW THE WING

WING

BIGGER WINGS

Move the hair-dryer away from the wing. The wing will not rise as easily.

LARGER AEROFOIL

FIRST AEROFOIL

You can also make a wing with a larger curved surface. This new wing will rise more easily because it creates more lift.

CONTROLLED FLIGHT

BIRDS AND AIRCRAFT CAN FLY IN A CONTROLLED WAY because they have movable surfaces. Birds use their wings and tail feathers, while aircraft have flaps. Build your own glider and see how these movable surfaces can affect the flight of your aircraft.

WHAT YOU NEED
Thin card
Double-sided tape
Drinks straw
Thin stick
Modelling clay

ROLL, PITCH AND YAW

Make your glider roll by moving the flaps on the wings. You can make your glider climb or dive (called pitch) by moving the flaps on the horizontal part of the tailplane. Make your glider move from side to side (yaw) by moving the flap on the upright part of the tailplane.

PITCH

ROLL

YAW

WHY IT WORKS

The lift created by the shape of the wings makes your glider fly. The movable surfaces turn the glider by deflecting the air as it flows over them. This deflected air pushes against the movable surfaces with enough force to alter the glider's course.

1 Cut out your wings and tailplane from card in the shapes shown. Cut out some thin strips of card which will be stuck to the wings and the tailplane. These will make the movable surfaces.

2 Fold the wings over and tape together to make an aerofoil shape (see pages 22-23). Feed a drinking straw through the wing to keep its aerofoil shape. Fold the tailplane into shape so that it looks like a 'T' when seen from the front.

3 Stick the thin strips of card in place on the back of each wing and also on the back of all three parts of the tailplane. Stick the wing on a thin stick, which will act as the glider's body. Attach the tailplane to a piece of a drinking straw and tape this onto the back of the stick.

4 Your glider should balance if it is rested on two cups by its wings. Add a lump of modelling clay to your glider's nose and change the amount until the glider balances evenly. Now you can fly your glider.

USING THE WIND

WHAT YOU NEED
Drinks carton
Drinking straws
Thin card
Wire
Ballpoint pen
Modelling clay

WINDS CAN BLOW VERY STRONGLY – hurricanes have caused lots of damage, uprooting trees and even demolishing houses! But winds can also be helpful. For hundreds of years, people have used the wind as a source of power to pump water up from deep wells or to grind wheat into flour. This experiment shows you how to build your own windmill and how it can harness the power of the wind.

WORKING WINDMILL

1 Make two sets of holes in either side of a drinks carton and feed two straws through them. The lower straw should point up towards the back of the carton.

2 Make two thin aerofoils (see pages 22-23) and thread a straw through both of them. Pierce the middle of the straw with the inside of a ballpoint pen.

3 Your windmill is going to turn a cam, which will push a hammer up. Cut out the shapes shown here from stiff card to make the cam, the hammer and a table which the hammer will hit.

BLOWING FROM ALL ANGLES

Try blowing on the blades of your windmill from different angles – in front, behind and to the side. You will find that the blades will turn quickest when you blow from the front.

BLOW
FROM BEHIND

BLOW FROM
THE SIDE

BLOW FROM
THE FRONT

4 Tape an L-shaped piece of wire to the back of the quarter circle to make the cam. Pierce a hole in the centre of the hammer, push another piece of wire through this and tape it into place. Now fold the head of the hammer over.

5 Push the inside of the ballpoint pen which is holding the blades of your windmill through the upper straw in the carton. Now feed the wire of the cam into the back of the pen's insides so that the cam spins with the blades.

6 Feed the hammer's wire into the lower straw. Fix some modelling clay to the head of the hammer and stick the table to the side of your windmill. Now blow on your windmill and watch the blades spin.

WHY IT WORKS

The blades of your windmill act as aerofoils (see pages 22-23). As air passes over them, they create lower pressure above the curved surfaces. The higher pressure below then pushes the blade up, causing the sails to turn.

DIRECTION
OF ROTATION

LIFT

FLOW
OF AIR

SAIL

LOW PRESSURE
ABOVE SAIL

IN A SPIN

WHAT YOU NEED
Thin card
Drinks straws
Modelling clay
Tape

WHILE NORMAL AIRCRAFT have fixed wings, some aircraft move their wings, spinning them around to produce lift. These aircraft, including helicopters, are called rotary-winged aircraft. Build your own rotary-winged aircraft, or whirligig, and find out how its spinning wings help it to fly.

MORE LIFT

Drop your whirligig and it will spin on its own as it falls. Now make the blades' angle steeper. You will find that the whirligig flies better.

4 *Hold the second straw between your hands with the blades uppermost. Now brush your hands together quickly to spin your whirligig and release it. Watch your whirligig spin as it flies.*

28

WHIRLIGIG

1 *Make two blades similar to the blades of your windmill (see pages 26-27).*

2 *Attach the straw running through the middle of the blades to another straw at a right angle using tape.*

3 *Fix a lump of modelling clay to the other end of the second straw. This will keep your whirligig upright as it flies.*

WHY IT WORKS

As the blades of your whirligig spin through the air, they act like aerofoils, creating low pressure above their curved surfaces (see pages 22-23). The high pressure below the blades pushes up, slowing the fall of your whirligig.

LIFT

LOW AIR PRESSURE ABOVE THE BLADES

DIRECTION OF SPIN

HIGH AIR PRESSURE BELOW THE BLADES

FINDING OUT MORE

AEROFOIL A special shape which is designed to rise when air flows over and under it. A wing is an aerofoil.

BAROMETER A device which measures changes in air pressure and is used to predict the weather.

DENSITY The heaviness of a substance for a particular volume.

EFFORTLESS FLYING

Gliders and hang-gliders don't need jet or propeller engines to fly. Instead, they use rising currents of warm air, called thermals, to lift them higher into the air.

DRAG Air resistance caused by disturbances in the flow of air over an object. This force slows down moving objects.

FRICTION A force that is created when two objects that rub together. It slows down the movement of these objects as they pass each other.

POWER LIFTER

The Mil Mi-26 Halo is the most powerful helicopter in the world today.

GRAVITY The attractive force between objects. The Earth's gravity keeps us on the ground.

EARLY CHOPPER

Over five hundred years ago, the Italian artist Leonardo da Vinci sketched the world's first helicopter – but it would have been too heavy to fly!

HOVERCRAFT A vehicle which moves about on a cushion of air.

LIFT An upward force which is caused by low air pressure above a surface.

PITCH The movement of an aircraft when the nose either rises or falls.

PRESSURE A force which is caused by the weight of the atmosphere.

ROLL The movement of an aircraft when one wing rises and the other falls.

STREAMLINED A streamlined object has a shape which helps it move through the air easily.

WIND The movement of air in the atmosphere.

WIND TUNNEL A device which is used to find out how streamlined objects are. It uses trails of smoke to see how air moves over the object's surfaces and how much drag the object creates.

YAW The movement of an aircraft when it turns either to the left or the right.

REED RAFT

In 1970, the explorer Thor Heyerdahl crossed the Atlantic Ocean in a wind-powered boat made from papyrus reeds.

INDEX